First World War
and Army of Occupation
War Diary
France, Belgium and Germany

58 DIVISION
175 Infantry Brigade
London Regiment
2/10 Battalion
2 September 1915 - 1 March 1916

WO95/3009/4

The Naval & Military Press Ltd
www.nmarchive.com
Published in association with The National Archives

Published by

The Naval & Military Press Ltd

Unit 10 Ridgewood Industrial Park,

Uckfield, East Sussex,

TN22 5QE England

Tel: +44 (0) 1825 749494

www.naval-military-press.com

www.nmarchive.com

This diary has been reprinted in facsimile from the original. Any imperfections are inevitably reproduced and the quality may fall short of modern type and cartographic standards.

© Crown Copyright
Images reproduced by permission of The National Archives, London, England, 2015.

Contents

Document type	Place/Title	Date From	Date To
Heading	WO95/3009/4/5		
Heading	58th Division 175th Infy Bde 2-10th Bn London Regt 1915 Sep-1916 Mar And 1917 Feb-1919 Mar		
Heading	WO95/3009/4		
War Diary	Woodbridge	02/09/1915	03/09/1915
War Diary	Bromeswell	04/09/1915	01/11/1915
War Diary	Ipswich	01/11/1915	01/03/1916

WO 95 30094
/5

58TH DIVISION
175TH INFY BDE

2-10TH BN LONDON REGT

~~FEB 1917 - MAR 1919~~

1915 SEP — 1916 MAR
AND
1917 FEB — 1919 MAR

WO 95
3009/4

Confidential

Monthly Statement

WAR DIARY
or
INTELLIGENCE SUMMARY

(Erase heading not required.)

2/10th London Regt

Army Form C. 2118

Instructions regarding War Diaries and Intelligence Summaries are contained in F.S. Regs., Part II. and the Staff Manual respectively. Title Pages will be prepared in manuscript.

Place	Date	Hour	Summary of Events and Information	Remarks and references to Appendices
Woodbridge	2/9/15		Unit — 2/10th Batt: London Regt.	
			Brigade 175th Brigade	
			Div 58th Division —	
			Mob. Cent 208 Mare Street, Hackney, N.E.	
			Demob War St — Woodbridge — Suffolk.	
			Stations Occupied — White City — Crowborough — Ipswich — Woodbridge —	
			(h) This unit is under the minimum strength of a draft supplying unit, and drafts cannot be obtained from the 3rd line Depot, thereby considerably hampering the training of the Battalion for Imperial Service.	
			Woodbridge 1/9/15	Vaughan ? Lt Col 2/10th London Regt

[Stamp: 58th (LONDON) DIVISION GENERAL STAFF 3 SEP 1915]

WAR DIARY or **INTELLIGENCE SUMMARY**

Army Form C. 2118

Confidential

1/5 2/10 Suffolk Regt

Place	Date	Hour	Summary of Events and Information	Remarks and references to Appendices
Woodbridge to BROMESWELL	Sept 2		Brigade Route March —	
	3		Removed to Bromeswell Camp —	
BROMESWELL	4		Blanket Inspection — Bn Parade —	
	5		Church Parade — Orders received for eight officers to embark for Mediterranean — left MELTON by 7.20 PM Train	
	6		Batt. Parade — B Co Construction of Musketry Range — D Co Bayonet Fighting Course — A + C Cos Training	
	7		Batt. Parade — B Co Construction of Musketry Range — B Co Bayonet Fighting C Co Entrenching — Aircraft alarm Troops turned out 8.15 PM —	
	8		A + B Cos marched to ALDERTON. Dinners in field — B Co Bayonet Fighting C Co Entrenching — Aircraft alarm Troops turned out 8.25 PM.	
	9		Training under Company arrangements — Aircraft alarm. Troops turned out 8.25 PM.	
	10		C + D Cos detailed to march to BAWDSEY (Cancelled) — Training under Company arrangements —	
	11		Training under Coy arrangements — Aircraft alarm Troops turned out 9.20 PM.	
	12		Church Parade — Aircraft alarm midnight Troops ordered to stand by. Zeppelin passed travelling N.E.	
	13		Training under Coy arrangements in morning — Bn Parade 1.45 PM. exercised in entraining at WOODBRIDGE Station. Aircraft alarm 7.50 PM. — Zeppelin passed S.W of Golf Club travelling E. Dropped several bombs. High explosive + incendiary about 3 miles away, — doing no damage —	
	14		Training under Coy arrangements —	
	15		" " " — Aircraft alarm. 8.10 PM —	
	16		" " " " —	
	17		A + B Co Training — C + D Coy to BAWDSEY. — Drivers in field — Aircraft alarm 11.15 PM Standby. by Cancelled. 11.55 PM.	
	18		Coy Training — Message from 175 Bn "Period of Vigilance Commenced" 7 PM —	
	19		Church Parade — Vigilance continued — Cancelled 3.20 PM —	
	20		Physical Drill — Coy Training Recruits Musketry —	
	21		Bn Training	
	22		Brigade Operations —	
	23		Brigade Route March —	
	24		Coy Training — Kit inspection — Feet inspection	
	25		Coy Training	

Army Form C. 2118

WAR DIARY
or
INTELLIGENCE SUMMARY
(Erase heading not required.)

Instructions regarding War Diaries and Intelligence Summaries are contained in F. S. Regs., Part II. and the Staff Manual respectively. Title Pages will be prepared in manuscript.

Place	Date	Hour	Summary of Events and Information	Remarks and references to Appendices
Oct. 26.	Sep 26		Church Parade ↓	
	27		Bt. Parade. Physical Drill. Co. Training ↓ 4 Officers 12 Selected N.C.O's Physical Drill Course ↓	
	28.		Bt. Training ↓	
	29.		Cos. Training ↓	
	30		Bt. 6.30 a.m Physical Drill – 9 am Trench Fighting ↓	
	Oct 1.		Bn. " " Assault Practice Bayonet Fighting Grenade	

Vansborough M.C.L
2/10 London Regt

Confidential

Army Form C. 2118

2/10th London Regt

WAR DIARY
or
INTELLIGENCE SUMMARY

(Erase heading not required.)

Instructions regarding War Diaries and Intelligence Summaries are contained in F. S. Regs., Part II. and the Staff Manual respectively. Title Pages will be prepared in manuscript.

3 - NOV. 1915
58th (LONDON) DIVISION
GENERAL

Place	Date	Hour	Summary of Events and Information	Remarks and references to Appendices
Bromeswell Camp	Oct 2		Bn. Parade 6.30am Physical Training. Bn. Parade. 9am., C Co Bayonet Fighting 9 – 11am II do 11 – 1 P.M.	
	" 3		Church Parade – ↓	
	" 4		Bn. 6.30am – 7.15am Physical Training – Bn. Parade 9.am. Company training – Bn. Parade 2.30 pm Co Training 2.30 to 4 P.M Co Training. Specialists trained 1.50 am ↓ – Specialists trained ↓ Aircraft alarm. Troops turned out 11.55 P.M returned 1.50 am ↓	
	" 5		Bn. 6.30am – 7.15am Physical Training – Bn. Parade 9.am Company training. 2.30 PM to 4 P.M. Co Training ↓ Specialists	
	" 6		" " " " " " " ↓	
	" 7		Brigade Route march – Specialists Carried on Training ↓	
	" 8		Bn. Physical Training. 6.30am – 7.15am. Bn. Parade 9am (Trenches) 2.30 P.M – 4 P.M. Co Training – Specialists to Carried on Training ↓	
	" 9		Physical Training 6.30am – 7.15 am. Company Training. 9am – 1 P.M. ↓. Corporal + Sication to 3/10 P.M. ↓	
	" 10		Church Parade – ↓	
	" 11		Physical Training 7.am to 7.45. Am – Bn. Parade 9am Coy Training – 2.30 P.M. – 4 P.M Co Training ↓	
	" 12		" " " " " " 9.30 am Trench Fighting – A + D Co Final Assault Practice 6.30 P.M ↓	
	" 13		Bn. Parade 8.30 am. Entrenching – Aircraft warning 7.35 P.M. Troops in position. Three Zeppelins passed came going E. One 11.40 P.M. Two 1.10am. Anti aircraft gun took up the first one while passing over Golf Club – ↓. Suspicious Signals in form of low trajectory rockets seen in direction of UFFORD MARSHES both at 11.40 P.M + 1.10 AM ↓ Troops returned 2.25 Am. ↓	
	" 14		Bn. Parade 9.30 am. A + D Co's Bayonet Fighting – A + D Co's 2.30 P.M – 4 P.M. Company Training B co 6.15–7 P.M Final C " 7pm – 7.45 Assault Practice ↓	
	" 15		Bn. Route march ↓	
	" 16		Company Training 9.30 AM – 1 P.M. – Physical Training 7.am – 7.45am ↓	
	" 17		Church Parade – ↓	
	" 18		Physical Training 7am to 7.45am, Bn. Parade 9am Co's 2.30–4 P.M. Co's 2.30 Cheer Death 2.30 P.M – 4 P.M. Semaphore – ↓	
	" 19		" " 1.10 P.M + " C + D Co's Final Assault Practice. 6.15 P.M – 7.45 P.M ↓ Normal 1.10 P.M + " " " Aircraft warning 10.10 am. Troops to stations Recure	
	" 20		Bn. Entrenching. Bus am to 1.30 P.M ↓	
	" 21		Route march ↓	
	" 22		Bn. Parade. 8.am. to Woodbridge Trenches. 200 rounds S.A.A per man. Inspection by G.O.C. Div. ↓	
	" 23		Physical Training. 7.am – 7.45am. Bayonet Fighting. A " 9am – 10.30am – B " 10.30am–12 noon, C " 6.15 P.M – 7 P.M. D " 7 P.M – 7.45 R ↓	

1875 Wt. W503/826 1,000,000 4/15 J.B.C. & A. A.D.S.S./Forms/C. 2118.

Army Form C. 2118

WAR DIARY
or
INTELLIGENCE SUMMARY

2/10 th London Regt

(Erase heading not required.)

Instructions regarding War Diaries and Intelligence Summaries are contained in F.S. Regs., Part II. and the Staff Manual respectively. Title Pages will be prepared in manuscript.

Place	Date	Hour	Summary of Events and Information	Remarks and references to Appendices
Bromeswell Camp	Oct 24th		Church Parade — L	
	" 25		Physical Training 7 am – 7.45 am. Bn. Parade 10.45 am. Entrenching at WOODBRIDGE – to 4 P.M. L	
	" 26		" " " " " 9 am to 1 P.M. Training – Night work. 6 P.M. – 8 P.M. Hotring + attacking Outpost line L –	
	" 27		Bn. Parade 8.30 am – 1.30 P.M. Entrenching – Aircraft alarm 9.10 P.M. Troops to Stations – Resume normal 11.55. P.M. L Nothing Seen L	
	" 28		Bn. Route March (Cancelled) as Very wet. Troops lectured in Camp. – L	
	" 29		Bn. Parade 7.45 am for Divisional Operations – returned 5.45 P.M. – L	
	" 30		Packing + loading Kits – Kit Inspection – Preparing for move. to Ipswich L	
	" 31		Church Parade —	
	Nov. 1st		Move to Ipswich for Winter Quarters L	

Bromeswell Camp.
1/11/15

Vansborough Lt Col
2/10 th London Regt

Confidential

Army Form C. 2118

2/10th London Regt

WAR DIARY
or
INTELLIGENCE SUMMARY
(Erase heading not required.)

Instructions regarding War Diaries and Intelligence Summaries are contained in F.S. Regs, Part II. and the Staff Manual respectively. Title Pages will be prepared in manuscript.

Place	Date	Hour	Summary of Events and Information	Remarks and references to Appendices
Ipswich	Nov/1/15		Moved into Ipswich from Bromeswell Camp —	
	2nd		Roll Call 6.45 a.m. Bn Parade 9.a.m - Inspection of billets by O.C. Companies in afternoon —	
	3		Roll Call 7.15 a.m. - Companies paraded independently 9 a.m. Specialists carry on training.	
	4		" 7.15 " Bn Parade Company drill - 9 a.m. under N.C.O's Tactical Exercises without Troops for Officers	
	5		10. a.m. — Company parade independently 2.30 P.m.	
	6		Roll Call 7.15 a.m Bn Parade 9 a.m. "A" Comp. Parade 1.45 P.m. for Inspection Sup; Gym; Staff. Qualified Instructor attend — Bn Parade 2.30 P.m — Corps + N.C.O's - Instructional drill —	
	7		Bn Parade 8.30 a.m. Training Blackheath Area —	
	7 1/2		Church Parade —	
	8		Bn Parade 8.30 a.m. Training - Brigade Commander Inspected Buildings 11 a.m — Trial Assault Practice 6 P.m (cancelled owing to course being under repair — Physical drill —	
	9		Bn Parade 8.30 a.m. Training. Senior N.C.O's Sketching under Maj; Pountney.. Company Parades 2.30 P.m —	
	10		Bn Parade 8.15 a.m. - Training - Physical drill etc —	
	11		Bn Parade 9.15. a.m. under Adjutant — Bn Parade 2.15 P.m. for Divisional Exercises at Stoke PARK,	
	12		Bn Field day (cancelled owing to rain) Officers + Sergts lectured by Maj: Pountney . Battn lectured by Capt Pratzlife	
	13		Bn Parade 8.45 a.m. Training Area G —	
	14		Church Parade —	
	15		Bn Parade 8.45 a.m. Training — Trial Assault Practice. 5.30 P.M. with 20 minutes interval between Companies	
	16		Bn Field day. Parade. 8.30 a.m Advance Gd + Attack on Position — Parade 3.30 P.m. Lecture on Morning work	
	17		Bn Parade 8.45 a.m. Training — Inspection of horses by Div; Remount Officer — 60 N.C.O's + men 4 days leave	
	18		Bn Parade 8.30 a.m Brigade Field Day	
	19		Bn " 9.15 a.m Physical Training, Kit Inspection + Pay in afternoon	
	20		" " 9 a.m Physical Inspection — Physical Training + Company drill 1 W.O + 3 Sergts attached to 3/10 Bn as instructors	

1875 Wt. W593/826 1,000,000 4/15 J.B.C. & A. A.D.S.S./Forms/C. 2118.

WAR DIARY
INTELLIGENCE SUMMARY

2/10th London Regt

Army Form C. 2118

Place	Date	Hour	Summary of Events and Information	Remarks and references to Appendices
Ipswich	Nov. 21st		Church Parade —	
	22nd		Company Training 8.45 am and 2.30 p.m — Final Assault Practice 5.30 p.m (Cancelled)	
	23rd		Inspection of Battn by Brigade Commander 11. am — Company training in afternoon —	
	24th		28 N.C.O's + men 14 days leave.	
			Bn Training 8.45. am Rushmere Heath — 5. Officers transferred to 3/10th —	
	25		Bn Parade 8.45 am Battn. Day Attack on Convoy — A. B + D Co. Capt Fenton Jones — "C" Coy (+ Convoy — Capt Bough) Parade 4.P.m for lecture on work done —	
	26th		Divisional Field Day	
	27th		Bn Parade 9am — 11 am — Company drill — Arm drill — Physical Exercises. 11.30 Kit Inspection —	
	28		Church Parade —	
	29th		Bn Parade 8.45 a.m Training Cos-Cs — Final Assault Practice 5.30 P.m. (cancelled owing not available) — lecture in afternoon —	
	30th		Bn Parade 9am — Reconnaissance for Brigade Scheme — lecture in afternoon —	
			Note — 2. Lieut Coffin + 28 men attended Refresher Machine Gun Course at Div. M.G. School Ipswich between Oct. 14th + Nov 30th —	
			Specialists carried on training daily except on Brigade + Divisional days.	

Ipswich
30/11/15

Vansborough Lt Col
2/10 London Regt

Confidential

WAR DIARY
or
INTELLIGENCE SUMMARY 2/10th London Regt.
(Erase heading not required.)

Army Form C. 2118

Instructions regarding War Diaries and Intelligence Summaries are contained in F.S. Regs., Part II. and the Staff Manual respectively. Title Pages will be prepared in manuscript.

Place	Date	Hour	Summary of Events and Information	Remarks and references to Appendices
Ipswich	13/12/15		Two Officers and 80 men to BOYTON, and One Officer + 25 men to CAPEL ST. ANDREW	
	17/12/15		Two Officers and 80 men returned from BOYTON, and One Officer + 25 men from CAPEL ST. ANDREW	
	19/12/15		One Officer and 27 men to CAPEL ST. ANDREW	
	23/12/15		One Officer and 27 men returned from CAPEL ST. ANDREW	
	28/12/15		One Officer and 12 men to WOODBRIDGE (for musketry) attached to 2/1st Bn.	

Vaursborough Lt Col.
2/10th London Regt

WAR DIARY 2/10th Batt. London Regt.
INTELLIGENCE SUMMARY

Army Form C. 2118

(Erase heading not required.)

Instructions regarding War Diaries and Intelligence Summaries are contained in F.S. Regs., Part II. and the Staff Manual respectively. Title Pages will be prepared in manuscript.

Place	Date	Hour	Summary of Events and Information	Remarks and references to Appendices
Ipswich	28/1/16	9.25 p.m	Battalion turned out for enemy aircraft Ok.	

Ipswich
1.2.16

C.I. Winkler
Capt Adjt
2/10 Bn London Regt.

Army Form C. 2118

WAR DIARY
INTELLIGENCE SUMMARY
(Erase heading not required.)

1/10th Bn London Regt.

Instructions regarding War Diaries and Intelligence Summaries are contained in F. S. Regs., Part II. and the Staff Manual respectively. Title Pages will be prepared in manuscript.

Place	Date	Hour	Summary of Events and Information	Remarks and references to Appendices
Ipswich	1/3/16		77 Army Recruits have been taken to strength during month of February	

C. L. Kempston
CAPT. & ADJT.
2/10th BATTALION LONDON REGIMENT.

www.ingramcontent.com/pod-product-compliance
Lightning Source LLC
Chambersburg PA
CBHW081514160426
43193CB00014B/2687